Learning Organisations

What they are and how to become one

Alan Clarke

NIACE

THE NATIONAL ORGANISATION
FOR ADULT LEARNING

Published by the National Institute of
Adult Continuing Education (England and Wales)
21 De Montfort Street
Leicester LE1 7GE

Company registration no. 2603322
Charity registration no. 1002775

NIACE, the national organisation for adult learning, has a broad remit to
promote lifelong learning opportunities for adults. NIACE works to develop
increased participation in education and training, particularly for those who
do not have easy access because of barriers of class, gender, age, race, language
and culture, learning difficulties and disabilities, or insufficient financial
resources.

NIACE's website on the internet is http://www.niace.org.uk

ISBN 1 86201 116 8

First published 2001
© 2001 National Institute of Adult Continuing Education (England and Wales)

Cataloguing in Publications Data
A CIP record for this title is available from the British Library

Designed and typeset by Boldface, London EC1
Printed and bound in Great Britain by Alden Press, Oxford

Acknowledgements

I would like to acknowledge the assistance provided by our partners in the Learning Organisation project (Leicester University, Centre for Labour Market Studies, Kevin Commons and Leicestershire TEC). Many individuals have also made significant contributions including Sue O'Hara, Elisabeth Baines, Stephen Hunt, Alice MClure, Ewa Rawicka, Munira Abdulhusein and Helen Biggs. I would like to thank Alice MClure for her reviews of many of the books in this field.

NIACE acknowledges that this publication would not have been produced without the support of Leicestershire Training and Enterprise Council.

Contents

Introduction

Many forces are changing the world in which we live, work and learn. This is not a recent development but it is one which is continuously accelerating. Many factors are causing this change but the critical ones are:

- the globalisation of markets;
- the impact of Information and Communication Technologies.

This new society requires individuals, communities and organisations to learn from their experience and to be continuously developing themselves. For individuals it is widely accepted that learning must become a lifelong process. It is no longer sufficient to complete your learning at school, you must be committed to learning throughout life.

In a similar way, organisations which do not learn from experience and take advantage of opportunities to develop themselves are likely to fail. Organisations are more than the sum total of their individuals. They are also teams of people, systems, processes and previous experience. Developing the individual is a critical factor in the success of any business but is not the end of the process. The organisation needs to be able to take advantage of the new knowledge and skills of the individual. Many individuals leave their employers because they feel constrained and stifled by the company structure. The organisation has failed to make the most of the individual.

To create an organisation that can take advantage of the new society requires a new type of organisation which can adapt to change, exploit opportunities and maximise the contribution of its human resources. This new type of business is often called a Learning Organisation. This guide is intended to help you consider the nature of a Learning Organisation and how to develop one within your own company.

2

What is a
Learning Organisation?

This is no one definition of a Learning Organisation. However, it is straightforward to identify the key characteristics that make a Learning Organisation. They are:

- Team-working and learning
- A culture of cross-organisational working
- A system of shared beliefs, goals and objectives
- Individuals, teams and an organisation which learns from experience
- Individual, team and organisational learning are valued
- Development of new ideas, methods and processes is encouraged
- Risk-taking is encouraged
- Responsibility and authority are delegated
- Everyone is encouraged and expected to perform to their maximum ability

---

Exercise 1. Duration: 30 minutes

Where are you?

1. Consider your own organisation and seek to answer the following questions.

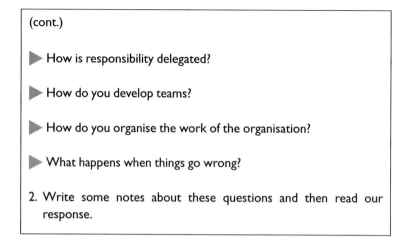

(cont.)

▶ How is responsibility delegated?

▶ How do you develop teams?

▶ How do you organise the work of the organisation?

▶ What happens when things go wrong?

2. Write some notes about these questions and then read our response.

Discussion

Exercise 1

There are no precise answers which say you are a Learning Organisation. However, if in your organisation authority is held by a small group of managers and everyone else works from their instructions, then you are likely to miss the opportunity to employ the skills, knowledge and experience of the staff fully. People are unlikely to see that it is part of their responsibility to make suggestions for improvements or even point out obvious errors when they are directed and instructed. Delegating responsibility encourages people to perform to the best of their abilities.

Often organisations train individuals but fail to realise that there is considerable need to consider the team. Team development is frequently assisted by everyone learning together; this is not suggesting that individual training is not critical but a Learning Organisation will consider both teams and individuals.

It is easy to structure work-flows so that teams and indiv-iduals work on only part of a process and are often unaware of what else happens. This can lead to teams and individuals being unaware of the consequences of their actions to other parts of the business as well as failing to see the opportunities of everyone being able to contribute to the success of the enterprise. In a fast-changing world you need to make the most of your most important resource – people. If you narrow their work and responsibility then you are wasting resources. A Learning Organisation encourages everyone to contribute with ideas and suggestions covering all parts of the business.

It is very easy to blame someone when things go wrong. It is their mistake so they should take the consequences. However, this is not likely to encourage people to accept responsibility, make suggestions about other parts of the company or have a go. Mistakes are opportunities to learn. They should be examined critically to learn how to prevent the error occurring again and to see if any benefit can be achieved. The culture of a Learning Organisation is to take acceptable risks – a culture of blame is not desired.

3

Benefits

The benefits of becoming a Learning Organisation include:

- being a flexible organisation which copes well with change;
- being an organisation which exploits the opportunities which new developments offer;
- improved and sustained productivity;
- reductions in costs;
- improvements in quality;
- being an organisation which learns from its errors.

A simple comparison of a traditional organisation and a learning organisation is given below (Table 1).

The essential difference is that a traditional organisation accepts limitations on its performance while a Learning Organisation aims to achieve a world-class standard of excellence.

Exercise 2   Duration: 5 minutes

Compare your own organisation to Table 1 and see if you can identify at which end of the spectrum it lies.

Traditional or Learning Organisation

Write some notes about this question and then read our response.

Table 1: Comparison of a traditional organisation with a Learning Organisation

Characteristics	Traditional organisation	Learning Organisation
Leadership	Director/instructor	Facilitator
Knowledge and skills	Specific expertise linked to distinct jobs	Expertise combined with excellent learning skills so that continuous self-development can be achieved
Organisational structure	Top-down	Flat structure with staff empowered to take initiatives
Staff	Fixed job descriptions	Responsibility delegated
Beliefs, goals and objectives	Achieve targets	Pursuit of excellence
Business plan	Fixed	Continuously developing
Measuring performance	Financially based	Includes many factors such as finance, organisational knowledge and human resources

Discussion

It is unlikely that your organisation will precisely fit either stereotype, but some aspects will be familiar. By comparing yourself to the Learning Organisation, you will be able to identify areas needing development.

4

How to become a Learning Organisation

There is no magic wand that will transform an organisation when you wave it. It is about a sustained effort over months and years which consists of many different actions. It requires the active participation of all the staff and their commitment to making the required changes. It is unlikely at the start of the process that you will know all the steps, detailed actions and outcomes that need to be achieved. The nature of a Learning Organisation is to allow everyone to contribute, which means things will change – including your initial plans for developing the Learning Organisation.

The key steps are likely to involve:

- Initial research
- Planning
- Launch
- Commitment from staff
- Changes in responsibility, processes and culture
- Review

Research

The initial step is almost certainly going to involve the consideration of the nature of your organisation and what you feel are its strengths and weaknesses.

Exercise 3　Duration: 30 minutes

SWOT Analysis

1. Using the simple grid below or something similar, list the strengths and weaknesses of your organisation and then the opportunities available to you and the threats your organisation faces.

2. Initially do not try to judge what items are more important than others. List everything even if you feel it is a relatively unimportant strength or a minor threat.

3. Once you have your lists, then attempt to identify which are important. A way of doing this is to grade each item as either 'must' items (those which you must address – i.e. they are essential to the business's development and survival); 'should' items (those which are important but could wait); and 'could' items (those which you would like to address if you ever have the resources).

Write some notes about these questions and then read our response.

SWOT

Strengths	Weaknesses
Opportunities	Threats

Discussion

Exercise 3

Once you have completed your own analysis ask your colleagues to repeat the process either individually or in a small group. Compare the different analyses and discuss the differences until you resolve them.

This process should provide you with an insight into the business and what needs to be done.

Planning

You need to plan how you are going to start and what processes you will initially employ. The nature of the Learning Organisation revolution is that the outcomes of these early steps are likely to change the process. However, spend some time considering the options. You need to involve people from all parts of the organisation and empower them to take things forward. This is likely to take time for people used to working in an environment where they are told what to do all the time. One approach is to establish a project team from all parts of the organisation to develop the plan. You may need to provide the team with external support to start the process.

In a Learning Organisation all activities should be seen as a learning opportunity and planning is no exception. Planning is sometimes seen as a production process with a defined product – the plan. However, planning is a learning process which is continuous in an organisation working within a climate of rapid change. That is, the plan continuously grows, changes and evolves.

Launch

A key feature of the Learning Organisation development is to communicate what is underway to everyone and to motivate individuals to make a positive contribution. This is most easily done with a launch event involving everyone.

Commitment from staff

A Learning Organisation will only be successful if the staff are committed to its goals and objectives. It is therefore vital from the first steps to involve them in all elements of the development.

Changes in responsibility, processes and culture

Learning Organisations are fundamentally about changing the culture and values of an organisation. It involves everyone accepting that the business must always be striving for excellence through revitalising and renewing the company. This is achieved through learning. Staff are free to contribute, try new ideas and openly debate approaches. This can be a dramatic change which will take time to achieve. One way to contribute to achieving these objectives is to change individual responsibilities. Some changes which have been used are:

- production workers given responsibility for scheduling work rather than supervisors;
- responsibility for quality given to workers rather than quality controllers;
- recruitment delegated to team managers while personnel are responsible for ensuring they are trained to do the task;
- award schemes and public recognition of success.

There is no ideal approach. You need to consider your own organisation and decide how to start. However, it is likely that you will need to introduce change over a period of months if not years. It is perhaps best to start with a small change in responsibility which affects most staff so that a clear early message is sent to everyone. It is important to study and learn from early steps.

Review

The plan, initial research, launch, commitment of staff and changes must be reviewed continuously since the whole process depends on learning from the experience.

5

Senior managers

There are significant differences between the roles of a senior manager in a conventional company and a Learning Organisation (Table 2). There is no single model for senior management behaviour in a Learning Organisation. The combination of factors is probably going to be unique to each manager. However, managers need to accept that the changes in the organisation which they are leading also means changes in their behaviour and styles.

Table 2: Senior managers' role

Conventional senior manager	Learning Organisation Manager
Manager first – leader second	Leader
Directs, instructs and orders	Facilitates and guides
Tend to be invisible	Highly visible
Judging	Helping people to think
Talks	Listens

During the development of a Learning Organisation, senior managers have a key role in bringing about the change. In fact they need to act as role models. In order to do this they need to be committed to the development, willing to challenge people, provide help and resources to enable people to achieve their learning goals and be far-sighted. The central issue is to encourage, support and develop learning within the organisation.

Exercise 4   Duration 30 minutes

Supporting learning

1. Consider how you could support learning within your own organisation and what methods are already used.

2. Write a list of possible methods and approaches.

Write some notes about these questions and then read our response.

Discussion

Exercise 4

There is a wide range of methods which can be employed within an organisation to encourage learning. These include:

- action learning – establishing a team to consider a particular problem with the objective of developing a solution, learning new skills and developing a new understanding of the issues. The whole team and the individuals are developed. This approach can be used to consider problems related to working towards the Learning Organisation;
- work shadowing – this can be a useful method of helping individuals to gain an insight into their new responsibilities or into the work of other parts of the organisation, thus aiding cross-team-working;
- learning centres – these can provide a focus for developing a

Learning Organisation and encourage individual responsibility for their own learning;
- short courses – intensive courses can be useful in developing knowledge and skills;
- open learning materials – these provide a means of offering learning in a flexible way so that the learner can choose where, when and at what pace to study;
- coaching – individual coaching can be a powerful way of aiding learning;
- mentoring – a useful way of assisting individual development;
- peer support – this is an especially valuable way in a climate of change and encourages team-working;
- feedback/discussion – this should include both positive and negative aspects but with an overall intention of being constructive.

No one learning method is a solution to all problems. They all have their own strengths and weaknesses. A key factor is that individuals have strong preferences for particular styles of learning. Some people like methods giving them many opportunities to be actively involved while other people like many opportunities to reflect on new experiences and knowledge. Some learners need to be able to see the whole subject before they can study the individual parts while others prefer to consider each individual section. Each learner will have his or her own unique mix of preferences. It is therefore important to employ a mix of methods.

Senior managers tend to concentrate on the financial management issues of the organisation. They are aware of costs, revenues, budgets and money but often less aware of the value to the organisation of its experience and knowledge. The critical resources of the human beings who staff the organisation are often not judged, while in a changing world they are frequently the major asset of the organisation.

In a Learning Organisation it is vital that senior managers are aware of and value the non-financial resources of the business, in particular the value of knowledge and people. A key advantage of a Learning Organisation is that each member of staff can contribute fully to the success of the enterprise.

Probably the majority of senior managers adopt a managerial style that which could best be described as controlled, planned, directed and constraining. This is probably effective in a stable environment with few significant changes but in the modern climate of considerable and continuous change it is no longer appropriate. The need is for staff who are flexible, adaptable and willing to learn. This culture will not be easily created in an organisation with an authoritarian culture.

6

Cross-team-working

Most organisations are highly structured, people work within defined areas and often have little contact with other teams. This fixed structure is fine within organisations which have little innovation or few changes. However, it is not providing an environment in which each member of staff can contribute fully to the success of the organisation or focus all its human resources on solving new problems. Organisations facing change need to have methods which allow all types of all their resources to be accessed and used to maximise the advantages of the change while minimising the risks.

A single team undergoing change may feel it is their responsibility to cope with and harness the change. However, since it is about change they may well not have the best mix of knowledge and experience available within the team. It is vital they can access all the available resources. A simple way is to establish a cross-team and multi-discipline project group to manage the change. This is a good approach assuming that the change is distinct and limited. However, in a climate of continuous development you need processes which allow for ongoing cross-team-working. This will involve:

- empowering everyone to offer suggestions and comments on all aspects of the business, not limited to their own responsibilities – without fear of recrimination;
- valuing everyone's ideas and removing any hierarchical bias

(such as managers being listened to more than workers);
- establishing a culture of mutual support;
- encouraging networking across the organisation.

Exercise 5   Duration 30 minutes

Analyse your organisation

1. Consider your own organisation and try to identify how often cross-team teams are formed to tackle problems.

2. Consider your own organisation and try to identify how often more informal cross-team-working happens.

3. What are the barriers to cross-team-working?

Write some notes about these questions and then read our response.

Discussion

Exercise 5

There are significant barriers to cross-team-working in most organisations. These include:

- Personal empires
- Difficulty in admitting you need outside help
- Being unaware what other teams can offer you
- Believing it is not your responsibility
- Unwilling to believe that solutions from other areas can be applied to your work (the 'not made here' syndrome)
- Blame culture – it is often easier to blame someone than admit you need help

- Job descriptions – useful in defining people's roles but they do tend to enclose and restrict individual initiative

7

Team-working and learning

A key element of a Learning Organisation is that teams both work and learn together. The importance of team development is not new. It is widely accepted that the sum of the individual efforts is less than that of the individuals combined in a team. Traditional team development has concentrated on helping the individuals fit together to form a coherent team to maximise their contribution to the organisation. This is still important but in a Learning Organisation a new priority is added: the need to develop a team which learns together.

There are many different sorts of team including:

- Project teams
- Functional teams

A project team is one which comes together for a distinct purpose such as solving a problem. Project teams feature in Learning Organisations, they aid cross-team-working and bring together the expertise of the whole organisation. A functional team is a permanent group which is trying to achieve common objectives (e.g. produce a product or provide a service). The needs of both types of groups are different but both need to learn.

How can a team learn? There are two main factors in team learning:

- Capturing the learning
- Reflecting on experiences

How can a team capture/record its learning? It is learning continuously and normally this is either lost or held in the memory of some of the individuals. The most straightforward method is to write down the knowledge. This has been done by teams producing detailed analyses of how to carry out tasks, keeping notes on experiences such as the different needs of customers, quality problems and how to resolve them and procedures for rare/occasional tasks. These types of records are very useful to aid the training of new team members, to develop quality assurance systems to meet external standards and to ensure that good practice is not lost. This type of knowledge can often be made available to the whole organisation by using intranets or shared resources of a systems network.

Keeping records of useful knowledge and experience will certainly help, but the team need to be given the opportunity to reflect on the learning in order to ensure everyone is aware of new material and also to build on the experience. Team meetings should be held regularly and a major feature of them should be to discuss experience, to allow new ideas to be suggested and for problems to be solved by the team. A culture of continuous improvement needs to be established. Problems are opportunities to learn, not to blame someone.

Some other useful techniques for team learning are:

- brainstorming – which can help develop more creative ideas and does assist with the initial introduction of team learning to break down barriers;
- using an external facilitator – who can help establish the process of discussing/reflecting on experience.

Exercise 6   Duration 30 minutes

Teams in your organisation

1. Consider your own organisation and begin to write a list of all the different teams and their functions.

2. How do teams capture their own experiences?

3. How are teams developed in your organisation?

Write some notes about these questions and then read our response.

Discussion

Exercise 6

You are likely to find that even in a small organisation there is a wide range of teams. Individuals are often members of more than one team. Some teams work in a defined area with a common purpose in which each person plays a role (e.g. assembling a product) so that if anyone is missing the objective cannot be achieved. Other teams are made up of individuals who work on their own (e.g. sales team). Some teams are very dispersed and rarely meet (e.g. managers across a site).

Experience is probably captured in a variety of ways. They will be inconsistent and will probably vary in effectiveness. Some common ways are:

- Day book where supervisors or team leaders record what has happened on their shift
- Quality control reports
- Customer records

- Customer complaints
- Minutes of meeting
- Successful proposals/tenders
- Unsuccessful proposals/tenders
- Production schedules
- Financial records – purchase orders
- E-mails, memos and other internal documents
- Individuals' notebooks to record contacts, useful ideas, conversion tables – anything they find useful

A great deal is recorded but a lot is lost. The information is widely scattered so that it is almost impossible to use it for continuous improvement. Individuals have access to most of the information while the team does not. Computer networks and intranets provide a means of rapidly accessing information. However, information needs to be removed, reflected on and discussed so that the lessons are identified.

Team development will vary from organisation to organisation but often there is very little apart from an occasional event. Managers may be sent away to take part in an outdoor exercise to help them work together. Isolated events are unlikely to achieve lasting results. Team development requires a coherent and long-term effort to succeed.

8

Shared beliefs, goals and objectives

It is a long-term task to change the beliefs, goals and objectives of individuals, teams and organisations. It is likely to take at least a year and more likely three or more years to achieve the change. External change can accelerate the process by providing overwhelming evidence that current culture needs to develop.

The key to developing a new basis for shared beliefs and values is involving each member of staff within the process of developing a Learning Organisation. Table 3 provides a comparison of communication methods and involvement.

Probably the most powerful influence on individual attitudes, beliefs and values is the team in which individuals belong and the organisation in which the team works. In reverse the way you change team views is through the individuals who make up the team. Some individuals are more influential than others and it is important to identify these change agents and target them to become the seeds for the changes in culture you are aiming to achieve. Influencers are often not the senior members of staff so aiming at managers and supervisors is not likely to be completely effective.

Table 3: Involvement and communication methods

Methods	Involvement
Noticeboard	Little personal involvement
Letter, note or memo	Some involvement if communication is personally addressed
Attitude surveys	Effective if it is clear that organisation acts on the results and they are available to everyone
Staff meeting	Can be useful if there is a significant opportunity for questions to be asked and answered. An effective meeting is one which allows a genuine dialogue between staff and management.
Staff consultation	Genuine consultation in all forms (e.g. small meetings, one-to-one discussion, focus groups, quality circles, etc.) has a high degree of involvement
Project teams	Cross-team groups meeting to solve a problem or enact change is highly participative
Cross-team-working	Continuous cross-team involvement through empowered staff
E-mail	Provides a means of allowing a dialogue but easy to be offensive unintentionally
Online mailgroups	Aids cross-team discussion

Exercise 7   Duration 30 minutes

Communication methods

1. Review the methods used to communicate with and gain the views of staff.

(cont.)

2. How effective are your current methods?

3. Produce your own table of methods and effectiveness.

4. How would you identify potential change agents?

Write some notes about these questions and then read our response.

Discussion

Exercise 7

Most organisations tend to base their communication on written messages, so have little potential for changing attitudes through these methods. Staff meetings are often one-way communication channels with little opportunity for a real dialogue.

Verbal messages are often cascaded through the management chain, which again has a limited impact. Few organisations attempt to identify influential members of staff and attempt to persuade them to assist the Learning Organisation development. In most groups it is often obvious who are the influential individuals simply because they are influential. They tend to stand out. They may not be obvious in the boardroom but each supervisor is likely to know who could be an agent for change.

9

Learning from experience
(individuals, teams, organisation)

A key factor in developing a Learning Organisation is to create a culture where all experiences are treated as learning opportunities. It is vital that any culture of blame is left behind. Taking calculated risks needs to be part of the organisation's culture. When mistakes are made, everyone takes advantage of an opportunity to learn. This is difficult to achieve in practice. There is little difference between a creative idea and a foolish error. To cope with a world of rapid and continuous change requires a distinct effort to achieve excellence through a workforce which can create, innovate and handle new situations. This is almost impossible to get right every time so when things go wrong the situation must be carefully analysed to gain the maximum benefit from the experience.

All experiences are opportunities for learning and people naturally learn from mistakes, but gaining the maximum benefit requires a systematic process. Some approaches are:

- Allowing time in every meeting for each person to say what they have learned since the last meeting
- Interviewing staff when they leave the organisation, to identify useful knowledge and experience
- Developing individual experience and helping cross-team-working by internal secondments
- Having review meetings to consider the organisation's performance on key projects

- Using coaches to aid individuals to review their own performance
- Using mentors to help individuals and teams to reflect on their experience
- Developing the learning skills of individuals

Exercise 8   Duration 30 minutes

Learning from experience

1. How does your organisation learn from experience, including errors?

2. How is experience shared across teams and the organisation?

Write some notes about these questions and then read our response.

Discussion

Exercise 8

Although organisations will frequently plan new projects or intiatives in a systematic manner, often establishing integrated project teams, relatively few put the same effort into reviewing the experience. There is a lot to gain from capturing the experience gained from a new development. If this is not done, when the next project arrives people will often be faced with limited memories of what was done and a lot of work has to be duplicated. This is a waste of resources and a recipe for repeating poor practice or reinventing wheels. At the end of each piece of work there needs to be a systematic examination of what happened. This will assist individual, team and organisational learning.

In this way every new project, development and order is a stepping stone to improved performance. Errors are therefore eliminated and good practice embedded. This process can be integrated into large projects by building in a regular pattern of review meetings, systematically recording decisions and their results and making it a normal event for individuals to openly discuss good and poor practice.

This process can be extended to cover everyday business so that it becomes an established feature of the way business is undertaken to review performance, not simply in terms of outcomes but also to reveal what can be learned from the work. The emphasis is on improvement and not limited to a discussion of outcomes.

10

Delegation of responsibility and authority

Most organisations are based on the concept of a hierarchy in which decisions are made at the top and implemented by managers and supervisors at different levels in the organisations. Responsibility is carefully defined and often centralised. By centralising responsibility and authority it is in effect disenfranchising whole groups of employees. If people do not have responsibility they have no incentive to contribute to the success of their work. This does not mean they do not work hard but sometimes they do not work as smartly as they could. Not involving staff is a waste of key resources. They have considerable experience to contribute which you are deliberately ignoring.

A major feature of a Learning Organisation is that you involve everyone in the pursuit of excellence. The key to participation is to give people a sense of ownership which can be achieved by systematically delegating responsibility to the appropriate staff. This should probably be accompanied by staff being given a direct reward linked to the success of the enterprise. In a commercial business this can take the form of profit-sharing schemes while in the public sector allowances for accepting particular responsibilities can be given. Voluntary organisations can offer public recognition (such as life membership).

Exercise 9

How would you begin the process of delegation?

Write some notes about this question and then read our response.

Discussion

Exercise 9

The delegation process will need to be accompanied with a training programme to ensure that staff have the knowledge and skills to carry out their new responsibilities. There is normally considerable scope for cost savings with this process as roles change and structures become less hierarchical. Where to start this process depends on individual organisations but some approaches are:

- Production workers are given responsibility for scheduling work
- Production workers are given responsibility for quality standards
- Team leaders are responsible for bonus payments
- Training is carried out by peers
- Office staff are responsible for ordering stationery and office equipment

Conclusions

Developing a Learning Organisation is not a small-scale or insignificant task. It will alter the fundamental nature of your organisation. It will not be achieved without a major effort over a long period (probably years). The outcome will be an organisation which can successfully cope with change in order to exploit opportunities to create a world-class organisation.

Appendix 1

Practical suggestions

Some practical suggestions to develop a Learning Organisation are:

* Senior managers must provide a role model
* Identify and employ influential members of staff as agents of change
* Treat each error as a learning opportunity
* Encourage cross-team-working
* Teams need to record their experience
* Teams must reflect on their experiences together
* Reward collaboration
* Encourage discussion across and within teams
* Ensure that systems exist to capture learning
* Review and document performance
* Encourage calculated risk taking and experimentation
* Delegate responsibility
* Ensure that people share in the success of the enterprise
* Value individual, team and organisational learning
* Communication is vital to ensure a culture of shared beliefs

Appendix 2

Useful contacts

Department for Education and Skills
http://www.dfes.gov.uk

National Institute of Adult Continuing Education (NIACE)
21 De Montfort Street, Leicester, LE1 7GE
http://www.niace.org.uk

National Training Organisations National Council
10 Meadowcourt, Amos Road, Sheffield, S9 1BX
http://www.nto-nc.org

Technologies for Training
32 Castle Street, Guildford, Surrey, GU1 3UW
http://www.tft.co.uk

Learndirect
http://www.ufiltd.co.uk

Learning and Skills Council National Office
101 Lockhurst lane, Foleshill, Coventry, CV6 5RS
http://www.lsc.gov.uk

Appendix 3

Information and communication technologies

There are a number of different communication technologies. They take two forms:

- Asynchronous
- Synchronous

Asynchronous technologies are methods which do not rely on the people being at either end of the communication channel. They include:

- e-mail (essentially one-to-one or one-to-many);
- bulletin boards (essentially many-to-many);
- bulletin boards (essentially one-to-many);
- intranet and internet websites;
- online conferences and seminars (one-to-one, one-to-many and many-to-many).

These approaches are widely used and would seem natural for improving communications.

Synchronous technologies are methods which do rely on the people being at either end of the communication channel. A telephone is a synchronous approach but leaving a message on an answer machine is asynchronous.

These approaches include:

- chat (a largely informal way of communicating of one-to-one and one-to-many and many-to-many);

- video- and audio-conferencing (essentially one-to-one and one-to-many);
- collaborative working using groupware (essentially groups of two or more people).

ICT can be a useful means of assisting the development of a learning organisation. However, it is only a tool and its effectiveness depends on how you employ it.

Comparison of Learning Organisation characteristics and ICT

Learning Organisation characteristics	Related communication technologies	Support
Team working and learning	E-mail	Aids communication between members of a team
	Groupware	Collaborative working
	Online conferences and seminars	Aid to cross-organisational learning
Cross-organisational working	E-mail	Aids cross-organisational communication
	Groupware	Collaborative working
	Intranet	Access to and dissemination of information

System of shared beliefs, goals and objectives	E-mail	Aids communication between members of a team
	Chat	Access to informal cross-organisational communication
Organisational memory	Intranet sites	Easy access to information
	Bulletin boards	Access to information
Learning from experience	Mailgroup	Cross-organisational communication
	Online conferences and seminars	Aid to cross-organisational learning
No-blame culture	Mailgroup	Cross-organisational communication
	Chat	Access to informal cross-organisational communication
Responsibility and authority is delegated	Intranet sites	Easy access to information
	Bulletin boards	Access to information
Staff performing to maximum ability	Intranet sites	Easy access to information
	Online conferences and seminars	Aid to cross-organisational learning
	E-mail	Support from colleagues

Appendix 4

Review of Learning Organisation books

Literature review: organisational learning and Learning Organisations

R. Lessem, *Business as a learning community: applying global concepts to organisational learning*, London: **McGraw Hill** (1991)
This is a philosophical text and a good read. Sections on management and leadership skills are worth a look. Lyall Watson´s analogy in which the pebble in the pond creates outward moving waves in concentric circles is used helpfully. If the crest of one wave coincides with the trough of another isolated patches of calm water are created – 'peace of mind' in this context with the individual at one with the job and giving quality performance. The section on self-assessment on learning and learning styles could be useful.

O. Nordhaug, *Human capital in organisations: competence, training and learning*, Oslo: **Scandinavian University Press** (1993)
Organisational competence and core competence of organisations are not purely analytical elements but are systems of parts that have to be interlinked to be effective. Thus there is need to configure an organisation's competence base. Most firms focus on provision, development, and utilisation of technical (task-related) competences. This narrow focus may be harmful usually because of need for over-arching competences.

Summary Points

Competence chain covers acquisition, development, utilisation and planning.

Technical competence does not prepare for change. Thus firms which concentrate their efforts on task specific competence may develop sclerosis and inertia.

R. Lessem, *Business as a learning community: applying global concepts to organisational learning*, London: McGraw Hill (1993) This establishes a social and economic context in which business, as a learning community, can be set up. The move from enterprise and management (which are materially-based resources) to an era of 'human capital' (which is knowledge-based) is discussed. It quotes Robert Reich (Bill Clinton's leading adviser). The key player in a nation's economy is neither a manager nor an entrepreneur, but a 'symbolic analyst' who iterates around four functions – abstraction, systems thinking, collaboration and experimentation.

Summary Points

Learning communities engage in:

* *information strategy;*
* *technology development;*
* *intellectual skill development;*
* *social system development.*

Reich's view, different to Senge (who focuses on individual managers), is that the whole is an interconnected enterprise web.

To create a learning organisation, conceptualise learning as a cycle.

Establish action learning sets.

Reconstitute organisation in layers of increasing complexity.

Orchestrate interdependence across the organisation.

Share communal knowledge.

M. Marquardt and A. Reynolds, *The global learning organisation; gaining competitive advantage through continuous learning,* **Richard D Irwin Inc** (1994)
Discusses global approaches to company improvement. There is no SME-related material though there is a quote commenting that size is a barrier to learning. There is often an indirect correlation between the size of the organisation and the amount of organisational learning.

W. W. Burke, *Organisation development: a process of learning and changing,* **Addison Wesley Publishing Company** (1994)
The text is about organisational development but Chapter 7 provides the Burke-Utwin model for analysis. It reminds the reader that any model being used for diagnosis should be:

- understood by practitioner/consultant;

- fit for the client organisation;

- sufficiently comprehensive to allow adequate data to be gathered.

B. J. Braham, *Creating a Learning Organisation: promoting excellence through education,* **Menlo Park Crisp Publications** (1995)
This series of self-paced open learning texts carry the 50 minute title. This book is of this style and meets some though not all of the requirements of open learning material. For example the various types of activity have banners but these are nowhere explained nor is the scoring system on the continuum exercises. Nonetheless, topics covered are comprehensive and if coverage is more declamatory than explanatory that is probably acceptable within the style of this publication. The first two parts cover the nature of Learning Organisations and the final two parts cover the responsibility for learning. Managing learning, learning styles and types are covered, barriers to learning, learning from good and bad experience and motivation likewise. The whole is a little like a romp through the subject but may be none the worse for that.

Summary Points

Tools are like bricks; they can be used to build a cathedral or a prison.

M. Pearn, C. Roderick, and C. Mulrooney, *Learning Organisations in practice*, London: McGraw Hill (1995)
This is a very accessible text. It draws on work carried out by the authors and others and provides a number of tools that organisations can use. It also sets these tools within a framework which explains, as you go along, the whys and wherefores of their use.

The book starts with helping organisations understand the implications of learning, goes on to consider how to categorise organisations in learning terms, then offers a working approach to becoming a learning organisation (hot-air-balloon analogy). There is a good section on analysing the state of learning in the organisation including tools to carry out a learning audit and to investigate the learning climate. The role of managers is covered followed by a section on the support and maintenance of learning with selected tools designed to facilitate learning. The final chapters are more reflective but provide some valuable insights.

Summary Points

Learning organisations set out to achieve the unattainable; it is the quest that is important, not the arrival.

M. H. Boisot, *Information space: a framework for learning in organisations, institutions and culture*, New York: Routledge (1995)
This text focuses on the indirect effects imposed on economic processes by information processes; effects mediated by cognitive, social, institutional and cultural structures, themselves also mediated by the encounter. Organisations are being transformed by new information technologies and the consequences and relationships are discussed. (May be useful for individual interest.)

S. Chawla and J. Renesch, *Learning Organisations*, Portland, Oregon: Productivity Press (1995)
Very academic text with essays from major researchers in the field.

C. Argyris and D. A. Schon, *Organisational learning II: theory method and practice*, New York: Addison Wesley Publishing Company Inc (1996)

This text provides a conceptual framework for organisational learning and for the relationship between research and practice. It introduces concepts central to limited learning and reviews the field. The reader presents controversial issues and challenges for consideration.

R. P. Mai, *Learning partnerships*, Chicago: Irwin Professional Publishing (1996)

This claims every organisation is a Learning Organisation. Quotes Argyris and Schon saying that there is no organisational learning without individual learning and that individual learning is a necessary but insufficient condition of organisational learning.

Provides case studies which some might find interesting.

Summary Points

Levels of learning:
Single loop v double loop (Argyris and Schon)
Adaptive v generative (Senge)
Operational v conceptual (Kim)
Superficial v substantive (Ulrich et al)

Barriers to learning: fear, control, success, conflict.

D. Casey, *Managing learning in organisations*, Buckingham, UK: Open University Press (1996)

Quite nicely written, fast paced text though a bit dense in places. Describes learning in groups, widened to organisations as a whole and discussion of organisation as a living entity – rather good. Examples from large companies.

R. Neilson, *Collaborative technologies & organisational learning*, London: Idea Group Publishing (1997)

This text sounds a warning note to those who think that throwing IT at a problem will work – Lotus Notes/groupware cited as example. The question is posed as to when downsizing, etc., companies may be left with the survivors and have, in fact, thrown away their intellectual capital.

G. Probst and B. Büchel, Organisational learning: *the competitive advantage of the future*, London: Prentice Hall (1997)
Introduces the need to consider the time factor – which is often ignored – in achieving Learning Organisation capability. Capacity to learn may be the critical resource of the future. It offers some case studies and work sheets for the process of becoming a Learning Organisation and suggests that the starting point should be to develop a learning model of the organisation.

R. Sanchez and A. Heene, *Strategic learning and knowledge management*, Chichester: John Wiley & Sons Inc (1997)
Examines the strategic management of knowledge and learning. Explores the competence perspective of learning and knowledge, learning processes within organisations and between organisations and looks at the strategic management of knowledge in competence-based competition.

P. Lassey, *Developing a Learning Organisation*, London: Kogan Page (1998)
The intention to integrate other UK initiatives including NVQs and Investors in People makes this text interesting and different. It is most likely to be of interest to those organisations already embarked upon some of those initiatives and seeking assurance or information as to their practice.

The book is not well served by its presentation as the reader may be put off by the density of the print.

M. Pedler and K. Aspinwall, *A concise guide to the Learning Organisation*, London: Lemos Crane (1998)
This is a fine text with activities and case studies clearly signposted. The way in which the various sections are integrated allows the reader to gain maximum benefit from the style of presentation.

There are good sections on learning and learning styles, barriers to learning is well covered and although the section on creating a learning organisation is quite short, the pointers offered have something for everyone.

Summary Points

Eleven characteristics of the learning organisation:
- *A learning approach to strategy*
- *Participative policy making*
- *Informating*
- *Formative accounting and control*
- *Internal exchange*
- *Reward flexibility*
- *Enabling structures*
- *Boundary workers as environmental scanners*
- *Inter-company learning*
- *A learning climate*
- *Self-development opportunities for all*

Organisation learning styles:
- *Habits*
- *Memory*
- *Modelling*
- *Experiment*
- *Enquiry*

K. E. Watkins and V. L. Marsick, *Sculpting the Learning Organisation*, San Francisco: Jossey-Bass Inc (1998)

This text could be useful for individual interest – the nature of continuous learning for individuals and how to design training to support individuals are discussed in sections two and three. Team learning, organisational learning and obstacles to learning are covered in some detail.

*Action **imperatives** for the learning organisation create:*

- *continuous learning opportunities;*

- *promote enquiry and dialogue;*

- *encourage collaborations and team learning;*

- *establish systems to capture and share learning;*
- *empower people toward a collective vision;*
- *connect the organisation to its environment;*
- *defining outcomes of a learning organisation;*
- *continuously learning;*
- *collaborative;*
- *creative;*
- *connective;*
- *collective;*
- *captured and codified;*
- *capacity building.*

M. Cope, *Leading the organisation to learn*, London: Financial Times Pitman Publishing (1998)

The relevant part of this text focuses on the use of particular models which bring together organisational learning and knowledge management.

P. Kline and B. Saunders, *Ten Steps to a Learning Organisation*, Arlington, Virginia: Great Ocean Publishers Inc (1998)

This text has in particular a section on how organisations learn. The set of assessment tools provided could be useful, as could some other sections of the text, if set alongside some of the other more useful material.

J. Denton, *Organisational learning and effectiveness*, London: Routledge (1998)

Provides case studies of five large organisations (3M, Coca Cola, etc.). Also some coverage of the public sector.

Summary Points

Characteristics of the Learning Organisation:

- Learning strategy
- Flexible structure
- Blame-free culture
- Vision
- External awareness
- Knowledge creation and transfer
- Quality
- Supportive atmosphere
- Teamworking.

Also p91.

J. R. Davis and A. B. Davis, *Effective training strategies: a comprehensive guide to maximising learning in organisations,* San Francisco: Berrett-Koehler Publishers Inc (1998)

The purpose of this book is to provide the reader with the capacity to make the most of learning in organisations through well established, theory-based training strategies which can be used to facilitate learning. The human characteristics most likely to facilitate learning are: life stage and developmental tasks; cognitive development; intelligence; aptitude and achievement; motivation and emotional intelligence; learning style; gender; ethnicity and social class.

B. Moingeon and A. Edmondson, *Organisational learning and competitive advantage,* London: Sage (1998)

This aims to bring together perspectives on strategy, organisational learning and development, both within management research. Part 1 examines knowledge and learning as contributors to competitive advantage, Part 2 examines the part resource in terms of competence and capability, and Part 3 describes the implementation of new strategies.

Summary Points

Organisational learning defined as:

- *Encoding and modifying routines*
- *Acquiring useful knowledge*
- *Increasing capacity to take productive action*
- *Interpretation and sense-making*
- *Developing knowledge about action outcomes*

J. B. Keys and R. M. Fulmer, *Executive development and organisational learning for global business*, New York: International Business Press (1998)
This begins by stressing the importance of thinking global to managers and leaders. It distinguishes between managers (who administer) and leaders (who bring about change). Global organisation needs to continually reinvent itself.

Summary Points

Quotes Marquardt (1996): Organisational learning includes five subsystems – learning, organisation, people, knowledge and technology.

Quotes Revans: learning must be greater than or equal to environmental change, or organisation will not survive.

Fortune magazine Learning Organisation is a consummately adaptive enterprise.

D. O. Ulrich, A. K. Yeung, S. W. Nason, and M. A. V. Glinoow, *Organisational learning capability*, Oxford University Press (1999)
This text is of the style of a consultant's handbook and provides examples of successful and unsuccessful organisations and provides copious worksheets and the like to use when working with organisations in defining and enhancing their learning capability.

Summary Points

Organisational learning capability is the capacity to generate new ideas with impact.

M. Easterby-Smith, J. Burgoyne, and L. Araujo, *Organisational learning and the Learning Organisation,* **London: Sage Publications Ltd** (1999)
Of particular interest here is the discussion of the need for the public sector to seek to become Learning Organisations. This sector is affected by the same pressures as the private sector; viz. Technology change, globalisation, competition. The public sector suffers additional pressure which may be described as internal in that it stems from the need to satisfy and justify their usefulness to their client base.

N. Kock, *Process improvement and organisational learning: the role of collaboration technologies,* **London: Idea Group Publishing** (1999)
Suggests process improvement as the focus for organisational learning and indicates the role of computer technology in the learning process. It defines data as a carrier of information and knowledge – information is descriptive, knowledge is associative.

Summary Points

Learning Organisations should establish an organisational culture that is conducive to knowledge creation and sharing.

J. G. March, *The Pursuit of organisational intelligence,* **Oxford: Blackwell Business** (1999)
The text straddles the divide between studies of how things happen in organisations and studies which advise organisations on how to improve. There are discussions on decision making in organisations and ideas are examined on how organisations learn and change, take risks and the complexities of advice giving and taking in organisations.

Summary Points

Organisations learn by encoding history into routines which guide behaviour.

The three classical behaviours which are observed as providing the basis of organisational learning studies: behaviours based on routine; actions that are history dependent; actions oriented to targets.

L. Argote, *Organisational learning: creating, retaining and transferring knowledge*, Boston: Kuwer Academic Publishers (1999)

Sets out to consider both organisational learning and forgetting along with the contribution, if any, to productivity of knowledge transfer within an organisation. The organisations studied produced aircraft, trucks and pizza.

Traditional learning curve shows time taken to produce a product decreases as experience of producers grow. However, the rate at which this learning occurs varies enormously. This text is written to summarise what is known about the factors which affect this rate: knowledge acquisition; transfer; and retention in organisations. Further studies recommended in particular on knowledge creation/acquisition.

D. R. Schwandt and M. J. Marquardt, *Organisational learning: from world class theories to global best practices*, Florida: CRC Press Ltd (2000)

This book presents 'a comprehensive model of organisational learning which will enable organisations to become deliberate and effective in learning, re-learning and un-learning'. It offers an analysis of the theories of organisational learning and suggests an Organisational Learning Systems Model (OLSM). The approach is very academic even in the presence of some examples (Whirlpool, IAM). It is however a useful text in terms of its contribution to the state of the art in this field today.

Summary Points

Learning Organisation = product

Organisational learning = process

Organisational learning is a system of actions, actors, symbols and processes that enables an organisation to transform information into knowledge. (Schwandt 1993)

1970s organisational learning may be single, double or dentor loop.

1980s four views of organisational learning as adaptive learning, assumption sharing, development of knowledge, institutional experience.

Organisational learning could be about either behavioural or cognitive change.

1990s and beyond, we move into open systems, chaos theory and the like thereby exposing higher orders of complexity.

OLSM and subsystems

New information/Environmental interface

Knowledge creation/Action – reflection

Structuring dissemination... diffusion

Sense-making... memory... meaning